Harford County Maryland
DIVORCE CASES

1827-1912

An Annotated Index

Henry C. Peden, Jr.

HERITAGE BOOKS
2007

HERITAGE BOOKS

AN IMPRINT OF HERITAGE BOOKS, INC.

Books, CDs, and more—Worldwide

For our listing of thousands of titles see our website
at
www.HeritageBooks.com

Published 2007 by
HERITAGE BOOKS, INC.
Publishing Division
65 East Main Street
Westminster, Maryland 21157-5026

International Standard Book Number: 978-0-7884-3551-5

FOREWORD

Genealogists often overlook divorce records in their search for family history, perhaps thinking a divorce never occurred in their family or perhaps not knowing where such records could be found. With this in mind, the late Mary Keysor Meyer published a book in 1990 entitled *Divorces and Names Changed in Maryland by Act of the Legislature, 1634-1867*. She noted that her abstracts of divorce cases had been copied from the published *Laws of Maryland*, a series of books found in numerous libraries in Maryland.

In early Maryland it took an act of the legislature to get a divorce. By the 1800's the increasing number of complaints placed a burden on the State that led to laws enacted in 1829, 1841, and 1853 which eventually delegated authority over divorce suits exclusively to the Courts of Equity in the various counties in Maryland. Meyer's book covers the cases heard by the Chancery Court for the State of Maryland, of which I found only 6 cases for Harford County before 1840. I then gleaned cases from the county's Court of Equity docket books between 1841 and 1912 and found over 300 more complaints.

The information abstracted was: names of the parties, case number, date of complaint, date of decree (if indicated), and any interesting comments noted in the docket books. In addition, I added many of the women's maiden names, dates of marriage, and dates of remarriage that I found in the marriage records of Harford County and Cecil County, plus some published marriage records from Baltimore City newspapers. Not all marriages, however, could be located, but I felt the annotations I made would be of help to researchers.

Oftentimes a decree of divorce *a mensa et thoro* (from bed and board, i. e., a legal separation) was granted, but not a divorce *a vinculo matrimonii* (final and absolute divorce decree). Sometimes a bill of complaint was filed, but not pursued, or dismissed, or perhaps re-filed later. My compilation is an annotated index to the divorce cases that I could find for Harford Countians between 1827 and 1912. One should consult the original files which contain the detailed information about the complaint before drawing any conclusions about any case listed in this index of divorces from the equity docket books.

Henry C. Peden, Jr.
707 Bedford Road
Bel Air, MD 21014

May 1, 1999

DIVORCE CASES, 1827-1912
HARFORD COUNTY, MARYLAND
A SUMMARY

Years	Number of Cases	Annual Average
1827-1829	1	.3
1830-1839	3	.3
1840-1849	6	.6
1850-1859	10	1.0
1860-1869	17	1.7
1870-1879	30	3.0
1880-1889	35	3.5
1890-1899	46	4.6
1900-1909	136	13.6
1910-1912	43	14.3

Total (1827-1912):   327 cases   avg. 4 cases per year

HARFORD COUNTY, MARYLAND, DIVORCE CASES, 1827-1912
AN ANNOTATED INDEX BY HENRY C. PEDEN, JR.

ACKERMAN, CLARA B., see "Taylor, Henry vs. Clara"

ACKINSON, ANNIE E. vs. ACKINSON, ALBERT P.
Case #6282, complaint filed 29 Sep 1905, decree issued 2 Jan 1906.
[Ed. Note: Albert P. Ackinson married Annie E. Duff on 13 May 1901.
Annie E. Eckinson *(sic)*, divorcee (age 19), married Joseph A. Barrett
(age 25), on 1 Jan 1906. Both marriages were in Harford County].

ADAMS, BLANCHE vs. ADAMS, EDWARD
Case #6510, complaint filed 18 Sep 1907, decree issued 18 Dec 1907.

ADAMS, FANNIE, see "King, Fannie vs. Rudolph"

ALLEN, RENA M. vs. ALLEN, ROBERT S.
Case #5164, complaint filed 20 Aug 1896, decree issued 14 Nov 1896.
[Ed. Note: Robert S. Allen married Rena M. Grafton by license dated
14 Feb 1885 in Harford County]. Also, an entry in the equity docket
book mentioned Baltimore City.

ALLENDER, CHARLOTTE A. vs. ALLENDER, JAMES
Case #5997, complaint filed 27 Apr 1903, but no decree was noted.

AMOS, EFFIE H. vs. AMOS, WILLIAM
Case #5860, complaint filed 20 Feb 1902, decree issued 22 Mar 1902.

AMOS, HENRY C. vs. AMOS, SARAH J.
Case #1842, complaint filed 13 Feb 1868, decree issued 15 May 1868.
[Ed. Note: Henry C. Amoss *(sic)* married Sarah Jane Whiteford by
license dated 20 Oct 1860 in Harford County].

AMOS, MARY vs. AMOS, ISAAC
Case #2157, complaint filed 14 Sep 1871, but no decree was noted.
[Ed. Note: Isaac Risteau Amoss *(sic)* married Mary Louisa Ault on
27 Nov 1860, as reported in the *Baltimore Sun* on 1 Dec 1860].

ANDERSON, GRACE vs. ANDERSON, WALTER F.
Case #5993, complaint filed 16 Apr 1903, decree issued 5 Jun 1903.
[Ed. Note: Walter Anderson married Grace Ashton on 26 May 1899
in Harford County].

ANDERSON, MARGARET, see "Askey, Robert vs. Margaret"

ANDREWS, EMMA L., see "Middleditch, William vs. Emma"

ASH, ALICE V. vs. ASH, ABRAM
Case #5822, complaint filed 19 Nov 1901, decree issued 23 Apr 1902.
[Ed. Note: Abram Ash married Alice Williams in Harford County by
license dated 30 May 1895].

ASHBRIDGE, SARAH E. vs. ASHBRIDGE, WINFIELD S.

2

Case #6608, complaint filed 17 Aug 1908, decree issued 1 Mar 1909.
[Ed. Note: Sarah Ashbridge, divorcee (age 30), married Daniel Barrow on 8 Jul 1909 in Harford County].

ASHTON, GRACE, see "Anderson, Grace vs. Walter"

ASKEY, ROBERT vs. ASKEY, MARGARET
State of Maryland's High Court of Chancery granted a divorce to Robert Askey from Margaret Askey on 17 Mar 1840. (This case is not listed in the equity docket of Harford County). [Ed. Note: Robert Askey married Margaret Anderson by license dated 2 Oct 1824 in Harford County].

AULT, MARY LOUISA, see "Amos, Mary vs. Isaac"

BACKSTER, SUSAN J. V., see "Johnson, Susan vs. Joseph"

BALDWIN, DEBBIE, see "Strong, Deborah vs. William"

BALDWIN, HANNAH E., see "Kazmier, Hannah vs. Andrew"

BALDWIN, MARY A., see "Stewart, Mary vs. Henry"

BALDWIN, ROSELLA, see "Busher, Ella vs. James"

BALDWIN, SARAH vs. BALDWIN, TYLER
State of Maryland's High Court of Chancery granted "femme sole" to Sarah Baldwin on 23 Feb 1841; it appears they had granted this "privilege" because Taylor *(sic)* Baldwin had "lost his mind, speech, etc." (This case is not listed in the equity docket for Harford County). [Ed. Note: Tyler Baldwin's medical problems were caused a stroke. He had married Sally Keen by license dated 20 Mar 1806 in Harford Co.]

BANKS, PROVY, see "Bond, Hannah vs. Alonzo"

BARNES, ELIZA, see "Murphy, Hester vs. John"

BARNES, GEORGE H. vs. BARNES, ELLEN N. COLLINS
Case #6248, complaint filed 12 Jun 1905, but no decree was noted. [Ed. Note: George Barnes (black) married Helen T. Collins (black) in Harford County by license dated 24 Oct 1894].

BARRETT, JOSEPH A., see "Ackinson, Annie vs. Albert"

BARROW, DANIEL, see "Ashbridge, Sarah vs. Winfield"

BATEMAN, LOUISE D. vs. BATEMAN, HARRY
Case #6956, complaint filed 22 Nov 1911, but no decree was noted.

BAUMGART, ANNA E., see "Skillman, Annie vs. Franklin"

BAVINGTON, JAMES C. vs. BAVINGTON, MARY M.
Case #2146, complaint filed 13 Jun 1871, decree issued 12 Feb 1874. [Ed. Note: James Bavington married Mary M. Baxter by license dated 30 Jan 1868, and James C. Bavingston *(sic)* married Mary E. Onion by license dated 22 Feb 1881, both times in Harford County].

BAXTER, MARY M., see "Bavington, James vs. Mary"

BAXTER, SUSAN J., see "Johnson, Susan vs. Joseph"

BAY, DANIEL A. vs. BAY, ELLEN G.
  Case #6526, complaint filed 9 Dec 1907, but no decree was noted.
  Case #6792, complaint filed 16 May 1910, decree issued 15 May 1911.
  [Ed. Note: Daniel Bay, widower (age 48), married Ellen J. *(sic)* Brown,
  widow (age 40), on 14 Jun 1906 in Harford County].
BAY, LAURA V. vs. BAY, WILLIAM
  Case #3816, "by her next friend Jackson Bennington"
  Complaint filed 9 Feb 1888, decree issued 28 Jul 1888.
  [Ed. Note: William Bay married Laura McFadden by license dated 17
  Apr 1865; she married second to Arthur Thomas, widower (age 51),
  on 6 Dec 1892; both times in Harford County].
BEALE, ANTOINETTE vs. BEALE, JAMES F.
  Case #5624, complaint filed 16 Jul 1900, dismissed 12 Nov 1900.
  Case #5780, complaint filed 23 May 1901, dismissed 11 Mar 1902.
  Case #6252, complaint filed 22 Jun 1905, decree issued 11 Jul 1905.
  [Ed. Note: James Beale married Antoinette Kehoe, widow (age 30),
  on 3 Nov 1897 in Harford County].
BECHTOLD, ERNESTINE vs. BECHTOLD, FREDERICK
  Case #6268, complaint filed 21 Aug 1905, but no decree was noted.
  [Ed. Note: Frederick Bechtold, widower (age 73), married Ernestine
  Krig, widow (age 38), on 3 Jul 1890 in Harford County].
BENNINGTON, JACKSON, see "Bay, Laura vs. William"
BENSKE, JOHN vs. BENSKE, MARY
  Case #6699, complaint filed 13 Jul 1909, decree issued 27 Dec 1909.
  [Ed. Note: John C. Benske, divorcee (age 38), married Julia Huatisak,
  of Baltimore, MD, by license dated 8 Apr 1910 in Harford County].
BENTLEY, CAROLINE, see "Connell, Caroline vs. Thomas"
BERRY, MOLLIE H., see "Bond, Mollie vs. James"
BEVANS, JOHN vs. BEVANS, REBECCA
  Case #2280, complaint filed 9 Jan 1873, decree issued 25 Feb 1873.
  [Ed. Note: John Bivans *(sic)* married Rebecca Smith by license
  dated 23 Apr 1868 in Harford County. It is interesting to note that a
  John "Bivans" married Hannah Johnson by license dated 8 Jan 1873,
  one day before John "Bevans" filed a bill of complaint for a divorce].
BILLINGSLEA, JAMES vs. BILLINGSLEA, MARTHA G.
  State of Maryland's High Court of Chancery granted a divorce to
  James Billingslea from Martha G. Billingslea on 6 Mar 1850. (This
  case is not listed in the equity docket book for Harford County.)
BILLINGSLEA, MARY A. vs. BILLINGSLEA, JACOB A.
  Case #5626, complaint filed 20 Jul 1900, decree issued 14 Dec 1900.

BILLINGSLEA, SUSAN E., see "Norris, Susan vs. John"

BILLINGSLEA, VICTORIA, see "Palmer, Victoria vs. John"

BILLMEYER, MARY ANNA, see "Swenson, Anders vs. Margaret"

BIRCKHEAD, JANE T. vs. BIRCKHEAD, SAMUEL H.
Case # 1188, bill of complaint for alimony filed on 17 Oct 1855, but dismissed per agreement 20 Jun 1856 (see next case below).

BIRCKHEAD, SAMUEL H. vs. BIRCKHEAD, JANE T.
Trans. from High Court of Chancery under Act of 1854, Chapter 183. Case #1173, filed 1 May 1855, dismissed per agreement, 20 Jun 1856. Case #1218, complaint filed 29 May 1856, decree issued 8 Jun 1856. [Ed. Note: Samuel H. Birckhead (relationship to above undetermined) married Sarah Rouse by license dated 13 Jan 1834 in Harford County].

BISHOP, SARAH, see "Waters, John vs. Sarah"

BIVANS, JOHN, see "Bevans, John vs. Rebecca"

BLUMENTRITT, THERESE V. vs. BLUMENTRITT, F. WILLIAM
Case #4455, complaint filed 12 Jul 1892, decree issued 27 Oct 1892.

BOARMAN, MARIA L., see "Forwood, Edward vs. Maria"

BODT, LIDY, see "Schirling, Lida vs. Michael"

BOLTON, HELEN T. vs. BOLTON, THOMAS J.
Case #5568, complaint filed 15 Jan 1900, but no decree was noted. [Ed. Note: Thomas J. Bolton married Teresa H. Laurue by license dated 9 Sep 1884 in Harford County].

BOND, CHARLES W. vs. BOND, REBECCA
Case #3164, complaint filed 13 Mar 1882, decree issued 18 Dec 1882. [Ed. Note: Charles W. Bond first married to Rebecca Giles by license dated 11 Jul 1871 and second to Christianna E. Bond by license dated 6 Jan 1883, both times in Harford County].

BOND, CHRISTIANNA E., see "Bond, Charles vs. Rebecca"

BOND, ELLA, see "Brown, Elbert vs. Ella (Nellie)"

BOND, HANNAH vs. BOND, ALONZO
Case #5907, complaint filed 14 Jun 1902, decree issued 30 Jan 1903. [Ed. Note: Alonzo Bond (black) married Hannah James (black) on 27 Nov 1894, and second to Provy Banks by license dated 26 Oct 1897, both times in Harford County].

BOND, HELEN M. vs. BOND, SAMUEL J.
Case #6157, complaint filed 14 Sep 1904, decree issued 8 Sep 1906. [Ed. Note: Samuel Bond (black) married Helen Milton Winters (black) on 31 Oct 1893 in Harford County].

BOND, MOLLIE H. vs. BOND, JAMES
Case #6288, complaint filed 14 Oct 1905, decree issued 5 Mar 1906.

[Ed. Note: James Bond (black) married Mollie H. Berry (black) in Harford County on 13 Sep 1899].

BOND, NANNIE vs. BOND, LENNOX B.
Case #5435, complaint filed 8 Oct 1898, but no decree was noted.
[Ed. Note: Lenox *(sic)* Bond married Annie Smith by license dated 31 Aug 1882 in Harford County].

BOND, REBECCA GILES, see "Bond, Charles vs. Rebecca"

BOONE, WILLIAM A. vs. BOONE, ANNIE ESTELLE
Case #6692, complaint filed 5 Jun 1909, decree issued 14 Oct 1909.
[Ed. Note: William Boone (black) married Estella Moore (black) in Harford County on 25 Feb 1904].

BOSLEY, LUCRETIA, see "Smithson, Thomas vs. Lucretia"

BOWER, JOHN W., see "Spath, Emily vs. John"

BOWMAN, J. HARVEY vs. BOWMAN, SARAH JANE
Case #5086, complaint filed 13 Apr 1896, decree issued 8 Aug 1896.
[Ed. Note: James H. Bowman married Sarah Jane Magee by license dated 29 Nov 1882 in Harford County].

BOYD, CAROLINE A. vs. BOYD, GEORGE H.
Case #5524, complaint filed 30 Aug 1899, decree issued 25 Jun 1901.

BRADFIELD, M. LILLIAN vs. BRADFIELD, ROBERT E. (G.?)
Case #6972, complaint filed 30 Dec 1911, decree issued 18 Feb 1913.
[Ed. Note: The marriage index stated Robert G. *(sic)* Bradfield (black) married Lillie M. Robinson in Harford County, but the marriage record on 15 Jul 1908 listed the name as "Robert G. Bradford (black)."].

BRADFORD, ALEXANDER, see "Strong, Deborah vs. William"

BRADFORD, ROBERT G., see "Bradfield, M. Lillian vs. Robert"

BRADLEY, LINGAN vs. BRADLEY, LUCY
Case #5955, complaint filed 21 Jan 1903, decree issued 21 Apr 1903.
[Ed. Note: Lingan Bradley (black), widower (age 47) married Lucy Matthews (black) by license dated 19 Oct 1895 in Harford County].

BRADLEY, SPENCER vs. BRADLEY, ELIZA E.
Case #5370, complaint filed 18 Feb 1898, but no decree was noted.
Case #6338, complaint filed 31 Mar 1906, decree issued 7 Sep 1914.
[Ed. Note: Spencer Bradley married Eliza E. Evans by license dated 26 Feb 1879 in Harford County].

BRADY, CASSANDRA vs. BRADY, FRANK
Case #5833, complaint filed 6 Dec 1901, decree issued 13 Jan 1902.
[Ed. Note: Frank Brady married Cassandra Brown by license dated 1 Jun 1871 in Harford County].

BRAINARD, VIRGINIA E., see "Walter, John vs. Virginia"

BROPHY, HANNAH E. vs. BROPHY, DENNIS
Case #4160, complaint filed 8 Aug 1890, "agreed" 22 Oct 1890.
Case #5520, complaint filed 17 Aug 1899, decree issued 9 Dec 1899.
[Ed. Note: Dennis Brophy married Lizzie Robinson by license dated
19 Dec 1885 in Harford County].

BROWN, AMELIA, see "Monk, Philip vs. Susan"

BROWN, CASSANDRA, see "Brady, Cassandra vs. Frank"

BROWN, ELBERT E. vs. BROWN, ELLA (NELLIE)
Case #5749, complaint filed 5 Mar 1901, but no decree was noted.
Case #6310, complaint filed 9 Jan 1906, but no decree was noted.
[Ed. Note: Elbert Brown (black) married Ella or Nellie Bond (black)
in Harford County on 17 Jun 1896].

BROWN, ELIZA vs. BROWN, THADDEUS
Case #6277, complaint filed 23 Sep 1905, decree issued 15 Oct 1906.
[Ed. Note: Thaddeus Stephens Brown (black) married Frances Eliza
Spencer (black) in Harford County on 26 Oct 1892].

BROWN, ELIZABETH vs. BROWN, JOHN C.
State of Maryland's High Court of Chancery confirmed the articles
of separation dated 24 Sep 1825, and on 29 Jan 1827 ordered them
to be recorded in the land records of Harford County with 6 months.
(This case is not listed in the equity court docket of Harford County).
[Ed. Note: John Brown married Elizabeth Morris Maulsby by license
dated 24 Feb 1808 in Harford County].

BROWN, ELLEN J., see "Bay, Daniel vs. Ellen"

BROWN, ISAAC vs. BROWN, ELIZA
Case #5853, complaint filed 5 Feb 1902, decree issued 23 Apr 1902.
[Ed. Note: Isaac Brown (black) married Eliza Rice (black) by license
dated 24 Jan 1888 in Harford County. It appears he may have married
first to Ella Reed by license dated 15 Dec 1894 in Harford County.
Additional research will be necessary before drawing conclusions].

BROWN, JEHU vs. BROWN, ELIZABETH
State of Maryland's High Court of Chancery granted a divorce to
Jehu Brown from Elizabeth Brown on 18 Feb 1848. (This case is
not listed in the equity docket book for Harford County).
[Ed. Note: Jehu Brown married Elizabeth Parmer by license dated
29 Dec 1824 in Harford Co.]

BROWN, LILLIAN A., see "Brown, Sarah vs. Simon"

BROWN, SARAH vs. BROWN, SIMON W.
Case #5247, complaint filed 3 Mar 1897, decree issued 1 Apr 1899.
[Ed. Note: Simon W. Brown married Sarah Gilpin by license dated

31 Jul 1876 in Harford County. On 20 Apr 1899 Simon W. Brown, of Dublin, MD, divorced (age 44), then married Lillian A. Brown, of Bel Air, MD, his widowed sister-in-law (age 25), in Harford County].

BUCHANAN, AMANDA E. vs. BUCHANAN, JOHN H.
Case #6842, complaint filed 3 Jan 1911, but no decree was noted.
[Ed. Note: John H. Buchanan (black) married Amanda Lee (black) in Harford County on 27 May 1888].

BUCHANAN, THOMAS vs. BUCHANAN, FRANCES J.
Case #6661, complaint filed 11 Mar 1909, decree issued 3 Apr 1911.

BURGESS, MARIAN, see "Preston, Marian vs. Samuel"

BURKINS, HATTIE M., see "Jones, Evans vs. Hattie M."

BURKINS, IDA BELLE, see "Cantler, John vs. Ida Belle"

BURTON, JONATHAN G. vs. BURTON, JOSEPHINE
Case #1882, complaint filed 7 Feb 1879, decree issued 2 Sep 1879.
[Ed. Note: Jonathan G. Burton, of Baltimore County, MD, married Josephine Lytle on 7 Mar 1868 in Harford County].

BURTON, JOSEPHINE vs. BURTON, JOHNATHAN GEORGE
Case #2660, complaint filed 4 Sep 1876, but no decree was noted.
[Ed. Note: Jonathan Burton married Josephine Lytle. See above case].

BUSHER, ELLA vs. BUSHER, JAMES F.
Case #5528, complaint filed 11 Sep 1899, decree issued 20 Mar 1900.
[Ed. Note: James Busher married Rosella Baldwin in Harford County by license dated 24 May 1888].

BUSHER, MARY ALICE vs. BUSHER, NICHOLAS W.
Case #5968, complaint filed 9 Feb 1903, decree issued 13 Oct 1903.
[Ed. Note: Nicholas Busher married Mary Wright in Harford County by license dated 19 Oct 1887].

BUTLER, SAMUEL F. vs. BUTLER, IDA S.
Case #6131, complaint filed 21 Jul 1904, decree issued 9 Aug 1904.
[Ed. Note: Samuel Butler (black) married Ida E. *(sic)* Harris (black) on 26 Jun 1902 in Harford County].

BUTTEL, WILLIAM B. vs. BUTTEL, CAROLINE
Case #5824, complaint filed 20 Nov 1901, dismissed 19 Sep 1902.

CADDELL, THERESA vs. CADDELL, THOMAS
Case #2030, complaint filed 18 Apr 1870, decree issued 10 Feb 1871.

CAHEN (COHEN?), LOUIS vs. CAHEN, ELIZABETH
Case #2581, complaint filed 27 Aug 1875, decree issued 10 Sep 1875.

CAMBURN, JOHN vs. CAMBURN, CLARA
Case #5940, complaint filed 17 Oct 1902, decree issued 10 Aug 1903.

CANTLER, GEORGE T. vs. CANTLER, HATTIE V.

Case #5698, complaint filed 3 Jan 1901, decree issued 17 Apr 1901.
[Ed. Note: George Cantler married Hattie V. Gray in Harford County
on 8 Mar 1896].

CANTLER, JOHN C. vs. CANTLER, IDA BELLE

Case #5803, complaint filed 28 Aug 1901, decree issued 12 Mar 1902.
[Ed. Note: John Cantler married Ida Belle Burkins in Harford County
on 10 Feb 1898].

CARLISLE (CARLILE), LEWIS M. vs. CARLISLE, ROSA E.

Case #5512, complaint filed 18 Jul 1899, but no decree was noted.
Case #5616, complaint filed 13 Jun 1900, decree issued 21 Dec 1900.
[Ed. Note: Lewis Carlisle married Rosa Gorman in Harford County
on 2 Jul 1892].

CARLISLE, NETTIE vs. CARLISLE, JOHN F.

Case #6722, complaint filed 25 Sep 1909. decree issued 18 Jul 1911.
[Ed. Note: John Carlisle married Nettie Cullum in Harford County by
license dated 6 Aug 1889].

CARR, MYRA S., see "Rigdon, John A. vs. Myra S."

CARROLL, LILLIE MAY vs. CARROLL, DANIEL H.

Case #6855, complaint filed 8 Feb 1911, dismissed 28 Nov 1913.
[Ed. Note: Daniel H. Carroll, son of James, married Lillie May
Derickson in Harford County on 23 Apr 1902].

CATSMEYER, ANDREW, see "Kazmier, Hannah vs. Andrew"

CHAMBERS, CORDELIA vs. CHAMBERS, WILLIAM

Case #2510, complaint filed 8 Dec 1874, decree issued 16 Jun 1875.
[Ed. Note: William Chambers married Delia Jackson in Harford County.
Cordelia Chambers married second to James L. Greenstreet on 21 Sep
1875, as reported in the *Baltimore Sun* on 25 Sep 1875. The marriage
license for James L. Greenstreett *(sic)* and Delia Chambers was issued
on 18 Sep 1875 in Harford County and the courthouse register states
they were married on 22 Sep 1875].

CHAMBERS, IRENE, see "Osborne, Irene vs. Benjamin"

CHAPPELL, ELIZA J. vs. CHAPPELL, GEORGE W.

Case #1725, complaint filed 30 May 1866, decree issued 16 Jan 1867.
[Ed. Note: George W. Chappell married Eliza J. Keene by license
dated 22 Jan 1863 in Harford County].

CHRISTY, HARRIET A., see "Draper, Edward vs. Harriet"

COALE, MARY A. vs. COALE, A. LEE

Case #7038, complaint filed 4 Jul 1912, dismissed 24 Jul 1912.
[Ed. Note: A. Lee Coale married Mary A. Jones in Harford County
by license dated 24 Feb 1883].

COHEN, ALICE vs. COHEN, JOSEPH E.
   Case #5754, complaint filed 18 Mar 1901, but no decree was noted.
COHEN, LOUIS, see "Cahen (Cohen?), Louis vs. Elizabeth"
COLE, EDA B. vs. COLE, HENRY A.
   Case #5543, complaint filed 30 Oct 1899, decree issued 19 Mar 1900.
COLE, EVA vs. COLE, ARCHER
   Case #6731, complaint filed 23 Nov 1909, but no decree was noted.
   [Ed. Note: Archer Cole (black), of Columbia, Pennsylvania, married
   Eva Moses (black) in Harford County, Maryland on 22 Dec 1903].
COLLINS, ELLEN N., see "Barnes, George vs. Ellen"
COLLINS, GEORGE H. vs. COLLINS, WINNIE
   Case #3990, complaint filed 11 Jun 1889, decree issued 19 May 1892.
   [Ed. Note: A George Collins married Levinia Gaines by license dated
   11 Oct 1876, and George H. Collins (black man, divorced) married
   Eliza C. White (black) on 6 Oct 1892, both times in Harford County.
   Additional research may be necessary before drawing conclusions].
COLLINS, HELEN T., see "Barnes, George vs. Ellen"
COLLINS, MARTHA vs. COLLINS, JAMES G.
   Case #6013, complaint filed 22 Jul 1903, decree issued 6 Nov 1903.
   [Ed. Note: James Griffith Collins married Martha Moore in Harford
   County by license dated 1 Aug 1895].
COLLINS, SUSAN vs. COLLINS, JOSEPH
   Case #2587, complaint filed 10 Sep 1875, but no decree was noted.
   [Ed. Note: Joseph G. Collins married Harriett S. Hilton by license
   dated 12 Feb 1868 in Harford County].
CONNELL, CAROLINE vs. CONNELL, THOMAS H.
   Case #4505, complaint filed 17 Jan 1893, but no decree was noted.
   [Ed. Note: Thomas H. Connell married Caroline Bentley by license
   dated 13 Aug 1883 in Harford County].
COURSE, JAMES vs. COURSE, MARGARET A.
   Case #2040, complaint filed 21 May 1870, decree issued 16 Aug 1870.
COX, ANNIE vs. COX, BENJAMIN
   Case #6422, complaint filed 14 Nov 1906, but no decree was noted.
   [Ed. Note: Benjamin Cox married Annie Spencer in Harford County
   on 26 Feb 1899].
CULLUM, ALBERT E. vs. CULLUM, MARTHA L.
   Case #3319, complaint filed 1 Feb 1884, decree issued 15 Apr 1884.
CULLUM, BESSIE MAY, see "Marshall, Bessie vs. George"
CULLUM, NETTIE, see "Carlisle, Nettie vs. John"
CUNNINGHAM, MARTHA E. vs. CUNNINGHAM, MORTIMER

State of Maryland's High Court of Chancery granted a divorce to
Martha Elizabeth Cunningham from Mortimer Cunningham on 27 Feb
1832 and ordered that she was to have custody of the children. (This
case is not listed in the equity docket for Harford County; however,
equity court case #521, on 14 May 1839, Mortimer Cunningham vs.
Sarah Ann Saunders, is recorded and pertains to the guardianship of
children). [Ed. Note: Mortimer Cunningham married Martha E. Dorney
by license dated 29 Oct 1827 in Harford County].

CURRY, FLORENCE, see "Few, Thomas vs. Florence"

CURRY, RALPH W. vs. CURRY, HANNAH E.
Case #2601, complaint filed 8 Dec 1875, decree issued 12 Apr 1876.
[Ed. Note: Ralph William Curry married Hannah E. Gate by license
dated 18 Dec 1867 in Harford County].

CURRY, SAMUEL vs. CURRY, MARTHA
Case #6873, complaint filed 22 Mar 1911, but no decree was noted.
[Ed. Note: Samuel J. Curry married Maggie L. Wright on 11 Jul 1888.
in Harford County].

CURTIS, MARY L. vs. CURTIS, JOHN E.
Case #6652, complaint filed 3 Feb 1909, decree issued 16 Jul 1909.

DANCE, CHARLES H. vs. DANCE, ANNIE BELLE
Case #6355, complaint filed 2 May 1906, decree issued 5 Jun 1906.
[Ed. Note: They apparently married again: Charles Dance, divorcee
(age 54) married Annie Belle Dance, divorcee (age 35), of Baltimore,
by license dated 14 Sep 1909 in Harford County].

DAUGHTON, LENA M., see "Walbeck, Henry vs. Lena"

DAVIS, E. VIRGINIA, see "Reed, Andrew vs. E. Virginia" and also
see "Reed, E. Virginia vs. Andrew"

DAVIS, MARY GRACE, see "Sharon, Margaret vs. John"

DAWSON, ELLA J., see "McFadden, Ella vs. William"

DAWSON, MARY S. vs. DAWSON, JOHN L.
Case #6359, complaint filed 17 May 1906, decree issued 24 Jul 1906.

DEAVER, SARAH A., see "Taylor, Sarah vs. Robert"

DEBAUGH, MARY C., see "Howlett, M. Katie vs. George R."

DECKMAN, P. W. vs. DECKMAN, LYDIA
Case #1757, complaint filed 29 Jan 1867, decree issued 25 Nov 1867.

DENNISON, JOHN T. vs. DENNISON, RACHEL V.
Case #6991, complaint filed 1 Mar 1912, but no decree was noted.
Case #7027, complaint filed 19 Jun 1912, but no decree was noted.
[Ed. Note: John T. Dennison married Rachel V. Monk in Harford
County by license dated 28 Jan 1901].

DERICKSON, LILLIE MAY, see "Carroll, Lillie vs. Daniel"

DILLWITH, JAMES, see "Dilworth, Mary vs. James"

DILWORTH, MARY C. vs. DILWORTH, JAMES
  Case #2189, complaint filed 1 Dec 1871, decree issued 23 Nov 1872.
  [Ed. Note: James Dillwith *(sic)* married Mary Scarborough by license
  dated 5 Mar 1866 in Harford County].

DORNAK, ANNIE FRANCES, see "Wright, William vs. Annie"

DORNEY, HARRIET vs. DORNEY, HENRY
  State of Maryland's High Court of Chancery granted a divorce to
  Harriet Dorney from Henry Dorney on 21 Mar 1837.
  [Ed. Note: Henry Dorney, Jr. married Harriott Woolen by license
  dated 6 Mar 1827 in Harford County].

DORNEY, MARTHA E., see "Cunningham, Martha vs. Mortimer"

DORSEY, ISAAC vs. DORSEY, AUGUSTA
  Case #5590, complaint filed 21 Mar 1900, decree issued 10 Jun 1901.
  [Ed. Note: Isaac Dorsey, widower (age 46) married Augusta Westcott
  in Harford County on 29 Jan 1893].

DORSEY, NELLIE E. vs. DORSEY, MAX HENRY
  Case #6272, complaint filed 31 Aug 1905, decree issued 19 Feb 1906.

DRAPER, EDWARD A. vs. DRAPER, HARRIET A.
  Case #6795, complaint filed 30 May 1910, but no decree was noted.
  [Ed. Note: Edward Draper (black) married Harriet A. Christy (black)
  on 12 Nov 1888 in Harford County].

DUFF, ANNIE E., see "Ackinson, Annie vs. Albert"

DUFF, ETTA, see "Tayson, Daniel vs. Etta"

DUNLEA, MAURICE vs. DUNLEA, IDA N.
  Case #6299, complaint filed 26 Oct 1904, decree issued 28 Dec 1905.
  [Ed. Note: Morris *(sic)* Dunlea married Ida N. Grafton on 20 Jun 1895
  in Harford County].

DURHAM, DAVID vs. DURHAM, MARY
  Case #1736, complaint filed 4 Aug 1866, decree issued 10 Feb 1868.
  [Ed. Note: David Durham married Mary A. Harker in Harford County
  by license dated 1 Apr 1864].

DURHAM, ROSE E., see "Hamilton, Grover vs. Oleita"

ECK, WILHELMINA vs. ECK, GOTTLIEB
  Case #4077, complaint filed 17 Jan 1890, dismissed 20 Sep 1890.
  [Ed. Note: Wilhelmina Eck, divorced (age 49), married Dayton B.
  Fisher on 23 Dec 1893 in Harford County].

ECKINSON, ANNIE E., see "Ackinson, Annie vs. Albert"

EICHOLZ, AMANDA A. vs. EICHOLZ, FREDERICK

12

Case #5445, complaint filed 9 Nov 1898, decree issued 2 Feb 1899.
[Ed. Note: Frederick Eichholtz *(sic)* married Amanda King in Harford County on 15 Apr 1891].

ELWOOD, ELLA M. vs. ELWOOD, MORRIS H.
Case #6771, complaint filed 28 Mar 1910, decree issued 15 Jul 1910.
[Ed. Note: An entry in the docket book mentioned Baltimore City].

ELY, WILLIAM T., see "Riley, Alice vs. William"

EMORY, GRISELDA vs. EMORY, THOMAS L.
Case #2748, complaint filed 13 Aug 1877, decree issued 2 Jan 1878.
[Ed. Note: Thomas L. Emory married Graselda Holmes by license dated 25 Oct 1864 in Harford County].

ENSOR, GEORGE B. vs. ENSOR, VIRGINIA H.
Case #6665, complaint filed 8 Apr 1909, decree issued 28 May 1909.

EVANS, ELIZA, see "Bradley, Spencer vs. Eliza"

EVANS, ELIZABETH, see "Thompson, William vs. Elizabeth"

EVANS, MURRELL vs. EVANS, MAMIE PEARL
Case #6623, complaint filed 27 Oct 1908, decree issued 23 Mar 1909.
[Ed. Note: Mamie Pearl Evans, divorcee (age 25), married William Schultz on 8 Apr 1910 in Harford County].

EVERETT, AMOS A. vs. EVERETT, HESTER H.
Case #2886, complaint filed 7 Feb 1879, decree issued 7 Apr 1879.
[Ed. Note: Amos A. Everett married Hester H. Grafton by license dated 22 Dec 1873 in Harford County].

FALLENBURG, EMMA, see "Frasch, Basil vs. Emma"

FEW, LYDIA, see "Lee, Lidie vs. Harry"

FEW, THOMAS HINKLE vs. FEW, FLORENCE M.
Case #5598, complaint filed 7 Apr 1900, decree issued 23 Jul 1900.
[Ed. Note: Thomas Hinkle Few married Florence Curry in Harford County on 26 May 1897].

FINK, LOUISA, see "Smith, William Abraham vs. Louise C."

FISHER, DAYTON B., see "Eck, Wilhelmina vs. Gottlieb"

FISHER, HARRY M. vs. FISHER, MARY IDA
Case #6174, complaint filed 15 Nov 1904, decree issued 3 Mar 1905.
[Ed. Note: Mary Ida Fisher (black), divorcee (age 37), of Steelton, Pennsylvania, married John C. Porter (age 30), of that same place, on 13 Aug 1909 in Harford County, Maryland].

FLETCHER, EMMA J. vs. FLETCHER, MOSES V.
Case #5747, complaint filed 5 Mar 1901, decree issued 31 Jul 1901.
[Ed. Note: Moses Fletcher (black) married Emma Tillman (black) in Harford County on 20 Jan 1895].

FLOWERS, LOUISA, see "Larue, Jacob vs. Sarah L."

FOARD, MARY ELIZA vs. FOARD, FRANCIS A.
Case #1082, complaint filed 28 Apr 1853, but no decree was noted.

FOREMAN, MARY, see "Robinson, Mary vs. Richard"

FORREST, MARGARET vs. FORREST, SAMUEL
Case #2866, complaint filed 30 Dec 1878, decree issued 23 Jan 1880.

FORWOOD, EDWARD vs. FORWOOD, MARIA LOUISA
Case #2929, complaint filed 9 May 1879, but no decree was noted.
[Ed. Note: Edward Forward *(sic)* had married Maria L. Boarman by
license dated 2 Sep 1857 in Harford County].

FRASCH, BASIL vs. FRASCH, EMMA
Case #3932, complaint filed 28 Jan 1889, decree issued 22 Mar 1902.
[Ed. Note: An entry in the equity docket book mentioned Baltimore
City. Basil Frasch had married Emma Fallenburg by license dated
13 Feb 1884 in Harford County].

FREEBURGER, MARY A. vs. FREEBURGER, GEORGE W.
Case #5215, complaint filed 23 Dec 1896, but no decree was noted.

FULFORD, ALEXANDER M., see "Walker, Sarah vs. Joseph"

GAINES, LEVINIA, see "Collins, George vs. Winnie"

GALLION, GARRETT E. vs. GALLION, GERTRUDE J.
Case #6829, complaint filed 28 Oct 1910, but no decree was noted.

GATE, HANNAH E., see "Curry, Ralph vs. Hannah"

GATES, ELIZA M. vs. GATES, LEVI T.
Case #6382, complaint filed 19 Jul 1906, decree issued 1 Sep 1906.
[Ed. Note: Levi T. Gates married Eliza Cullum in Harford County
on 10 Jan 1895].

GATES, LEVI T. vs. GATES, ELIZA C.
Case #5684, complaint filed 26 Nov 1900, but no decree was noted.
[Ed. Note: Levi T. Gates married Eliza Cullum. See above case].

GEARY, NINA, see "Jewens, Nina vs. Marvin"

GIBSON, ELIZABETH vs. GIBSON, WILLIAM
State of Maryland's High Court of Chancery granted a divorce to
Elizabeth Gibson from William Gibson on 17 Feb 1827. (This case
is not listed in the equity docket book for Harford County.)

GIBSON, ETTA vs. GIBSON, WILLIAM
Case #6801, complaint filed 28 Jun 1910, but no decree was noted.
[Ed. Note: William Gibson (black) married Etta Jones (black) in
Harford County on 2 May 1903].

GIBSON, SARAH, see "Williams, Samuel vs. Sarah"

GILBERT, GEORGE WILSON, see "Gilbert, Martha vs. George"

14

GILBERT, GIDEON vs. GILBERT, CLEMENCY
Case #1515, complaint filed 10 Jun 1861, decree issued 12 Apr 1863.
[Ed. Note: Gideon Gilbert married first to Clemency Mitchell by license dated 9 Apr 1856 and married second to Rachel A. Gilbert by license dated 27 Feb 1865, both times in Harford County].

GILBERT, EVELYN, see "Michael, Evelyn vs. Jacob C."

GILBERT, LAVENIA, see "Giles, Samuel vs. Levinia"

GILBERT, MARTHA M. vs. GILBERT, GEORGE WILSON
Case #5748, complaint filed 5 Mar 1901, decree issued 27 Aug 1901.
[Ed. Note: George W. Gilbert married Martha M. Gilbert in Harford County on 30 Jan 1888].

GILBERT, RACHEL A., see "Gilbert, Gideon vs. Clemency"

GILES, REBECCA, see "Bond, Charles vs. Rebecca"

GILES, SAMUEL EDWARD vs. GILES, LEVINIA
Case #6326, complaint filed 22 Feb 1906, but no decree was noted.
[Ed. Note: Samuel E. Giles married Lavenia (sic) Gilbert in Harford County on 18 Apr 1879].

GILPIN, SARAH, see "Brown, Sarah vs. Simon"

GLENN, ANGY J. vs. GLENN, ROBERT J.
Case #6716, complaint filed 9 Sep 1909, but no decree was noted.
[Ed. Note: Robert Glenn, widower (age 56), married Angeline Grove (age 25) in Harford County on 14 Dec 1905].

GOANS, LILLIE, see "Holland, Agnes vs. Oliver"

GONZALES, JOSE vs. GONZALES, FLORENCE
Case #6505, complaint filed 15 Aug 1907, decree issued 12 Mar 1909.
[Ed. Note: Jose Gonzales, of Reckord, Maryland, widower (age 45), married Florence Eva Hitchcock in Harford County on 9 Mar 1904].

GORDON, J. PEARL, see "Kroh, George vs. J. Pearl"

GORMAN, ROSA E., see "Carlisle, Lewis vs. Rosa"

GOVER, ELEANOR C. vs. GOVER, HARRY
Case #6969, complaint filed 27 Dec 1911, decree issued 12 Apr 1912.

GOVER, HARRY vs. GOVER, ELEANOR H.
Case #6728, complaint filed 8 Nov 1909, dismissed 1 Nov 1911.

GRAFTON, HESTER H., see "Everett, Amos vs. Hester"

GRAFTON, IDA N., see "Dunlea, Maurice vs. Ida N."

GRAFTON, RENA M., see "Allen, Rena vs. Robert"

GRAFTON, SARAH R. vs. GRAFTON, JOSEPH T.
Case #1732, complaint filed 11 Jul 1866, decree issued 18 Feb 1867.
[Ed. Note: Joseph Grafton married Sarah R. Saunders by license dated 28 Sep 1857 in Harford County].

GRAY, HATTIE V., see "Cantler, George vs. Hattie"

GRAY, MAMIE, see "Stump, Mamie vs. Elmer"

GRAY, MARGARET JANE, see "Robinson, Richard vs. Margaret"

GREENSTREET, JAMES L., see "Chambers, Cordelia vs. William"

GRIFFITH, ABBIE M. vs. GRIFFITH, WILLIAM H.
   Case #5432, complaint filed 17 Sep 1898, decree issued 3 Jul 1899.
   [Ed. Note: William Griffith, of Baltimore, Maryland, married Abbie
   Pennington in Harford County on 25 Apr 1895].

GROVE, ANGELINE, see "Glenn, Angy vs. Robert"

GROVER, ALICE P. vs. GROVER, CHARLES H.
   Case #3718, complaint filed 7 Feb 1887, decree issued 26 Feb 1887.

HAINES, INDIA, see "James, William vs. India"

HALL, ASIA, see "Wade, Asia vs. Stewart"

HALL, HANNAH, see "Stewart, Alexander vs. Hannah"

HALL, SALLIE, see "Preston, John vs. Sarah"

HAMILTON, GROVER H. vs. HAMILTON, OLEITA M.
   Case #6693, complaint filed 5 Jun 1909, decree issued 9 Dec 1909.
   [Ed. Note: Grover H. Hamilton married Oleita M. Herrman on 24 Jun
   1904, and Grover H. Hamilton, divorcee (age 29), married second to
   Rose E. Durham on 20 Mar 1916; both times in Harford County].

HANNA, EDITH S. vs. HANNA, J. HOWARD
   Case #5358, "by her next friend George L. Van Bibber"
   Complaint filed 31 Dec 1897, dismissed(?) 26 Mar 1898.
   Case #5648, complaint filed 14 Aug 1900, decree issued 4 Sep 1900.

HANNA, J. HOWARD vs. HANNA, ANNA BELLE
   Case #4005, complaint filed 27 Jul 1889, decree issued 1 Jun 1897.
   [Ed. Note: J. Howard Hanna married Anna B. Preston by license
   dated 24 Aug 1881 in Harford County].

HANNAN, RICHARD T. vs. HANNAN, KATIE VIRGINIA
   Case #6115, complaint filed 23 May 1904, decree issued 7 Nov 1904.
   [Ed. Note: Richard Hannan married Katie V. Johnson on 12 Aug 1886
   in Harford County].

HARKER, MARY A., see "Durham, David vs. Mary"

HARMAN, JACOB vs. HARMAN, LOUISA
   Case #1206, complaint filed 4 Apr 1856, decree issued 26 Jan 1857.

HARRIS, GEORGE, see "Stump, Mamie vs. Elmer"

HARRIS, IDA E., see "Butler, Samuel vs. Ida"

HARRIS, MARY, see "Spriggs, William vs. Mary"

HARSON, RUBY vs. HARSON, CHARLES
   Case #6481, complaint filed 6 May 1907, decree issued 24 Jun 1908.

HAVILAND, EDWIN vs. HAVILAND, MARY L.
   Case #3929, complaint filed 22 Jan 1889, decree issued 22 May 1889.
HEDRICK, EMMA M., see "Knight, Emma vs. John"
HERRING, CHARLES H. vs. HERRING, JEMMIMA
   Case #1998, complaint filed 29 Jan 1870, but no decree was noted.
   [Ed. Note: An entry in the docket mentioned Wilmington, Delaware].
HERRMAN, OLEITA, see "Hamilton, Grover vs. Oleita"
HICKS, MARY ELIZABETH vs. HICKS, JOHN
   Case #6243, complaint filed 23 May 1905, decree issued 15 Aug 1905.
HICKS, SARAH E. vs. HICKS, JAMES THOMAS
   Case #6684, complaint filed 13 May 1909, decree issued 26 Oct 1909.
   [Ed. Note: James T. Hicks married Sarah E. Osborn on 30 Apr 1898
   in Harford County].
HIGGINS, JOHN F., see "Wilder, Mary vs. William"
HILL, ALFRED, see "Hilton, Alfred vs. Alice"
HILL, FANNIE W., see "Hilton, Fannie vs. Henry"
HILL, HANNAH E. vs. HILL, RALPH C. (H.?)
   Case #3359, complaint filed 26 May 1884, decree issued 1 Sep 1884.
   [Ed. Note: Ralph H. *(sic)* Hill married Hannah Smith by license dated
   14 Dec 1876 in Harford County].
HILL, WILLIAM H. vs. HILL, ELIZA
   Case #3750, complaint filed 28 Apr 1887, decree issued 30 Apr 1888.
   [Ed. Note: William Henry Hill married Eliza E. Kell by license dated
   4 Sep 1873 in Harford County].
HILTON, ALFRED B. vs. HILTON, ALICE
   Case #6862, complaint filed 28 Feb 1911, decree issued 22 May 1911.
   [Ed. Note: Alfred Hilton, widower (age 40), married Ella Williams (age
   23) on 3 Jan 1901 (index listed his name as "Hilton," but the entry of
   marriage mistakenly gave his name as "Hill"). Alfred B. Hilton (black),
   divorcee (age 40), married Nealy E. Webster (age 28) on 25 May 1911.
   Both marriages were in Harford County].
HILTON, FANNIE W. vs. HILTON, HENRY O.
   Case #6451, complaint filed 25 Jan 1907, but no decree was noted.
   [Ed. Note: Henry O. Hilton (black) married Fannie W. Hill (black) in
   Harford County on 30 Nov 1899].
HILTON, HARRIET S., see "Collins, Susan vs. Joseph"
HILTON, PHOEBE, see "Williams, Phoebe vs. John"
HITCHCOCK, FLORENCE, see "Gonzales, Joses vs. Florence"
HOFFMAN, ALLEN vs. HOFFMAN, MINERVA
   Case #2732, complaint filed 28 May 1877, decree issued 29 Sep 1877.

[Ed. Note: Allen Hoffman then married Sallie R. Sheridan by license dated 28 Nov 1877 in Harford County].

HOFFMAN, ELIZABETH HELEN, see "Pontier, Elizabeth vs. Charles"

HOLLAND, AGNES A. vs. HOLLAND, OLIVER S. JR.
Case #4894, complaint filed 11 Jun 1895, but no decree was noted.

HOLLAND, OLIVER S. vs. HOLLAND, AGNES A.
Case #5490, complaint filed 18 Apr 1899, decree issued 1 Aug 1899.

HOLLEY (HOLLY), MARY E. vs. HOLLEY, WILLIAM W.
Case #2848, complaint filed 24 Oct 1878, but no decree was noted.
Case #3165, complaint filed 14 Mar 1882, decree issued 20 May 1882.

HOLLINGSWORTH, SUSAN, see "Ringgold, Eliza vs. Emory"

HOLMES, GRASELDA, see "Emory, Griselda vs. Thomas"

HOOPMAN, MARY, see "Palmer, Charles vs. Mary"

HOPKINS, JESSE J. vs. HOPKINS, EMMA J.
Case #4331, complaint filed 17 Aug 1891, dismissed(?) 9 Nov 1891.

HOPKINS, RACHEL, see "Lytle, Rachel vs. James"

HOWLETT, M. KATIE vs. HOWLETT, GEORGE R.
Case #6415, complaint filed 25 Oct 1906, but no decree was noted.
[Ed. Note: George Howlett married Mary C. Debaugh on 18 Feb 1891 in Harford County].

HUATISAK, JULIA, see "Benske, John vs. Mary"

HUGHES, BERTHA MAY vs. HUGHES, DAVID R.
Case #6025, complaint filed 28 Aug 1903, but no decree was noted.

INGRAM, SARAH H. vs. INGRAM, MICHAEL
Case #4316, complaint filed 26 Jun 1891, decree issued 9 Sep 1892.

JACKSON, DELIA, see "Chambers, Cordelia vs. William"

JAMES, HANNAH, see "Bond, Hannah vs. Alonzo"

JAMES, WILLIAM E. vs. JAMES, INDIA A.
Case #5987, complaint filed 26 Mar 1903, decree issued 25 Jul 1904.
[Ed. Note: William E. James (black) married India A. Haines (black) on 2 Feb 1894 in Harford County].

JAMISON, SADIE, see "Robinson, Daniel vs. Sadie"

JANNEY, MARGARET A. vs. JANNEY, ASBURY
Case #6403, complaint filed 3 Sep 1906, decree issued 2 Jan 1907.
[Ed. Note: Asbury Janney, of Baltimore County, widower (age 69), married Margaret (Maggie) Whiteford, widow (age 59), in Harford County on 16 Apr 1902].

JEMISON, LOUISA C. vs. JEMISON, MARTIN
Case #4247, complaint filed 4 Feb 1891, decree issued 26 May 1891.

JEMMISON, SARAH ANN, see "Robinson, Daniel vs. Sadie"

JEWENS, HELEN, see "Smith, William A. vs. R. Helen"
JEWENS, NINA J. vs. JEWENS, MARVIN G.
  Case #7047, complaint filed 31 Jul 1912, decree issued 10 Sep 1912.
  [Ed. Note: Marvin Jewens married Nina J. Geary in Harford County
  on 30 Nov 1899].
JOHNS, ELIZABETH vs. JOHNS, RUDOLPH
  Case #1357, complaint filed 20 Jan 1859, decree issued 7 May 1861.
JOHNSON, FLORENCE R., see "Johnson, Rebecca vs. William"
JOHNSON, HANNAH, see "Bevans, John vs. Rebecca"
JOHNSON, KATIE V., see "Hannan, Richard vs. Katie"
JOHNSON, REBECCA vs. JOHNSON, WILLIAM E.
  Case #6812, complaint filed 16 Aug 1910, but no decree was noted.
  [Ed. Note: W. Elmer Johnson married Florence R. Johnson on 23 Dec
  1891 in Harford County].
JOHNSON, SADIE, see "Shipley, Sadie vs. Albert"
JOHNSON, SUSAN J. vs. JOHNSON, JOSEPH
  Case #2354, complaint filed 29 Jul 1873, decree issued 17 Jan 1874
  [Ed. Note: Joseph Johnson married Susan J. V. Backster by license
  dated 5 Dec 1867 in Harford County].
JOHNSON, WILLIAM THOMAS vs. JOHNSON, JENNIE E.
  Case #6879, complaint filed 5 Apr 1911, but no decree was noted.
  [Ed. Note: William Thomas Johnson married Jennie Evelyn Wells in
  Harford County on 7 Nov 1898].
JONES, E. FLORENCE vs. JONES, HUGH E.
  Case #6580, complaint filed 16 May 1908, dismissed 16 Jun 1908.
JONES, EDWARD W. vs. JONES, LILLIAN
  Case #6872, complaint filed 21 Mar 1911, but no decree was noted.
  [Ed. Note: An entry in the docket book mentioned Baltimore City].
JONES, ETTA, see "Gibson, Etta vs. William"
JONES, EVANS L. vs. JONES, HATTIE M.
  Case #6981, complaint filed 22 Jan 1912, decree issued 29 Jan 1912.
  [Ed. Note: Evans L. Jones married Hattie M. Burkins on 20 Nov 1907
  in Harford County].
JONES, JACOB F. vs. JONES, DAISY H.
  Case #6603, complaint filed 7 Jul 1908, decree issued 27 Aug 1908.
  [Ed. Note: Jacob F. Jones married Daisy H. Pyle in Harford County
  on 4 Nov 1897].
JONES, JOSHUA D. vs. JONES, ELIZABETH ANN
  Case #898, complaint filed 19 Dec 1850, but no decree was noted.
JONES, MAGGIE J., see "Whiteford, Joseph vs. Margaret"

JONES, MARY A., see "Coale, Mary vs. A. Lee"

JORDAN, MOLLIE A., see "Stine, George vs. Mary"

KAZMIER, HANNAH ELIZA vs. KAZMIER, ANDREW
Case #3891, complaint filed 12 Nov 1888, decree issued 18 Feb 1889.
[Ed. Note: Andrew Catsmeyer *(sic)* married Hannah E. Baldwin by
license dated 23 Jan 1872 in Harford County].

KEEN, SALLY, see "Baldwin, Sarah vs. Tyler"

KEENE, ELIZA J., see "Chappell, Eliza vs. George"

KEHOE, ANTOINETTE, see "Beale, Antoinette vs. James"

KEITH, JOHN H. vs. KEITH, SARAH
Case #3677, complaint filed 8 Oct 1886, decree issued 22 Dec 1886.
[Ed. Note: John H. Keith married Sarah Welsh by license dated
25 Feb 1879 in Harford County].

KELL, ELIZA, see "Hill, William vs. Eliza"

KELLY, FANNY, see "Carroll, Lillie vs. Daniel"

KENLY (KENLEY), GERTRUDE O. vs. KENLY, E. LARKIN
Case #7018, complaint filed 1 Jul 1912, but no decree was noted.

KENLY, KATE FLORENCE vs. KENLY, LAWSON H.
Case #3510, complaint filed 13 Aug 1885, decree issued 7 Dec 1885.

KENLY, MARY A., see "Murphy, John vs. Mary"

KING, AMANDA, see "Eicholz, Amanda vs. Frederick"

KING, FANNIE A. vs. KING, RUDOLPH
Case #5614, complaint filed 7 Jun 1900, but no decree was noted;
it also indicated "Rudolph King sometimes called Rudolph Kuhn."
[Ed. Note: Rudolph King married Fannie Adams by license dated
6 Mar 1876 in Harford County].

KING, MARGARET vs. KING, TIMOTHY
Case #4023, complaint filed 3 Oct 1889, but no decree was noted.

KNIGHT, EMMA M. vs. KNIGHT, JOHN S.
Case #6449, complaint filed 24 Jan 1907, but no decree was noted.
[Ed. Note: John S. Knight married Emma M. Hedrick on 23 Feb 1888
in Harford County].

KNIGHT, HARRIETT vs. KNIGHT, WILLIAM V.
Case #2150, complaint filed 6 Jul 1871, decree issued 14 Dec 1871.

KNIGHT, SARAH OLIVIA vs. KNIGHT, WILLIAM C.
Case #6887, complaint filed 24 Apr 1911, decree issued 21 Aug 1911.

KRIG, ERNESTINE, see "Bechtold, Ernestine vs. Frederick"

KROH, GEORGE W. vs. KROH, J. PEARL
Case #6831, complaint filed 31 Oct 1910, decree issued 29 May 1911.
[Ed. Note: George William Kroh married J. Pearl Gordon on 19 Sep

1900 in Harford County].

KUHN, RUDOLPH, see "King, Fannie vs. Rudolph"

LANOIR, ANDREW vs. LANOIR, MARIAN
Case #5992, complaint filed 15 Apr 1903, decree issued 31 Aug 1903.

LARUE, JACOB D. vs. LARUE, SARAH L.
Case #6011, complaint filed 1 Jul 1903, but no decree was noted.
[Ed. Note: Jacob D. Larue, of South Delta, Pennsylvania, married
Louisa Flowers in Harford County on 16 Aug 1896].

LARUE, MARY C., see "Silk, Mary vs. John"

LAURUE, TERESA H., see "Bolton, Helen T. vs. Thomas"

LEE, ALICE L. vs. LEE, WILLIAM D.
Case #6281, complaint filed 28 Sep 1905, decree issued 16 Jan 1906.
[Ed. Note: William D. Lee married Alice L. Standiford on 20 Jul 1898
in Harford County].

LEE, AMANDA, see "Buchanan, Amanda vs. John"

LEE, CATHARINE SWIFT, see "Temple, Benjamin vs. Alice"

LEE, LIDIE vs. LEE, HARRY W.
Case #6695, complaint filed 10 Jun 1909, but no decree was noted.
[Ed. Note: Harry W. Lee married Lydia Few in Harford County on
5 Nov 1904].

LEGAR, MARY E., see "Wise, Mary vs. Daniel"

LEGOE, SALATHIEL vs. LEGOE, ELIZABETH J.
Case #1478, complaint filed 17 Jan 1861, decree issued 11 Nov 1862.
[Ed. Note: Salathiel Legoe married an Ellen Roberts by license dated
28 Dec 1838 in Harford County].

LEWIS, DAVID J. JR. vs. LEWIS, MARY A.
Case #3715, complaint filed 4 Feb 1887, decree issued 22 Mar 1888.

LEWIS, ELIZA A., see "Ringgold, Eliza A. vs. W. Emory"

LEWIS, THOMAS W. vs. LEWIS, CATHARINE A.
Case #4039, complaint filed 7 Nov 1889, but no decree was noted.

LOGAN, MARY, see "Walker, Sarah vs. Thomas"

LYLE, EDNA G., see "Ray, Edna vs. Eugene"

LYNCH, JOHN G. vs. LYNCH, CATHERINE McVEY
Case #5570, complaint filed 20 Jan 1900, decree issued 2 Oct 1900.

LYTLE, JOSEPHINE, see "Burton, Jonathan vs. Josephine"

LYTLE, RACHEL vs. LYTLE, JAMES
Case #790, complaint filed 9 Dec 1846, but no decree was noted.
[Ed. Note: James Lytle married Rachel Hopkins by license dated
10 May 1831 in Harford County].

MACATEE, THOMAS B., see "McAtee, Ruth vs. Thomas"

MACKIN, JOSEPH L. vs. MACKIN, ELIZABETH HATTIE
   Case #5429, complaint filed 8 Sep 1898, decree issued 8 Jul 1899.
   [Ed. Note: Joseph L. Mackin married Lizzie H. Wilkinson by license
   dated 25 Jul 1881 in Harford County].
MAGEE, SARAH J., see "Bowman, J. Harvey vs. Sarah Jane"
MARKU, WILLIAM vs. MARKU, HENRIETTA
   Case #5790, complaint filed 9 Jul 1901, decree issued 20 Mar 1902.
   An entry in the equity docket book mentioned Baltimore City.
   [Ed. Note: A William Marku, widower (sic), age 45, married Annie
   Watters, of Cecil County, Maryland, widow (age 32), on 3 Jul 1906
   in Harford County].
MARSHALL, BESSIE M. vs. MARSHALL, GEORGE W.
   Case #6777, complaint filed 9 Apr 1910, decree issued 18 Sep 1911.
   [Ed. Note: George William Marshall married Bessie May Cullum in
   Harford County on 11 May 1905].
MATTHEWS, LUCY, see "Bradley, Lingan vs. Lucy"
MAULSBY, ELIZABETH M., see "Brown, Elizabeth vs. John"
MAXWELL, CLARA vs. MAXWELL, DAVID
   Case #4515, complaint filed 9 Feb 1893, but no decree was noted.
McATEE, RUTH E. vs. McATEE, THOMAS B.
   Case #1639, complaint filed 6 Apr 1864, but no decree was noted.
   [Ed. Note: Thomas B. Macatee married Ruth E. Streett by license
   dated 10 Jan 1853 in Harford County].
McCALL, THOMAS vs. McCALL, FLORENCE
   Case #3138, complaint filed 28 Dec 1881, decree issued 22 Jun 1882.
   [Ed. Note: Thomas McCall married first to Florance Stittartt in 1874
   in Cecil County, Maryland in 1874. Thomas T. McCall married Belle
   Wright by license dated 13 Nov 1882 in Harford County].
McCANN, CARRIE, see "Swift, Robert E. vs. Carrie V."
McCOMAS, LOUISA, see "Moore, Mark vs. Belle"
McCOMMONS, Florence, see "Youmans, Florence vs. George"
McEWING, MOLLIE, see "Walker, Alonzo vs. Mary Ann"
McEWING, SEVANION vs. McEWING, EDNA
   Case #6124, complaint filed 1 Jul 1904, decree issued 19 Sep 1904.
McFADDEN, ANNIE S. vs. McFADDEN, OTIS S.
   Case #5846, complaint filed 10 Jan 1902, decree issued 10 Nov 1902.
   [Ed. Note: Ottis (sic) S. McFadden married Annie S. Taylor in Harford
   County on 26 Feb 1883].
McFADDEN, ELLA J. vs. McFADDEN, WILLIAM T.
   Case #4988, complaint filed 28 Oct 1895, decree issued 3 Feb 1896.

[Ed. Note: William T. McFadden married Ella J. Dawson by license dated 5 Apr 1886 in Harford County].

McFADDEN, LAURA V., see "Bay, Laura vs. William"

McGONIGALL, E. MAY vs. McGONIGALL, ALBERT S.
  Case #3200, complaint filed 19 Sep 1882, decree issued 28 Apr 1883.

McNABB, JOHN vs. McNABB, HENRIETTA
  State of Maryland's High Court of Chancery annulled the marriage and granted a divorce to John McNabb, of Baltimore City, from Henrietta McNabb, of Harford County, on 10 Mar 1847. (This case is not listed in the equity docket book for Harford County).

McNABB, SARAH B. vs. McNABB, WILLIAM
  Case #1235, complaint filed 2 Feb 1857, decree issued 26 May 1857.

MICHAEL, EVELYN A. vs. MICHAEL, JACOB CALVIN
  Case #6864, complaint filed 6 Mar 1911, but no decree was noted.
  [Ed. Note: J. Calvin Michael married Evelyn A. Gilbert on 21 Jun 1904 in Harford County].

MICHAEL, JAMES W. vs. MICHAEL, MARGARET E.
  Case #2376, complaint filed 10 Sep 1873, decree issued 27 Sep 1873.
  [Ed. Note: James W. Michael married Mary E. Stockham by license dated 15 Mar 1864 in Harford County].

MIDDLEDITCH, WILLIAM T. vs. MIDDLEDITCH, EMMA L.
  Case #4011, complaint filed 2 Aug 1889, decree issued 16 Jun 1891.
  [Ed. Note: William T. Middleditch married Emma L. Andrews by license dated 1 Nov 1883 in Harford County].

MITCHELL, CLEMENCY, see "Gilbert, Gideon vs. Clemency"

MOFFETT, DORA, see "Thalman, Fred vs. Dora"

MOFFETT, STELLA, see "Shay, George vs. Stella"

MONK, PHILIP H. vs. MONK, SUSAN
  Case #2624, complaint filed 5 Apr 1876, decree issued 8 Sep 1876.
  [Ed. Note: Philip H. Monk then married Amelia Brown by license dated 9 Sep 1876 in Harford County].

MONK, RACHEL V., see "Dennison, John vs. Rachel"

MOORE, ESTELLA, see "Boone, William vs. Annie E."

MOORE, MARK vs. MOORE, BELLE
  Case #6052, complaint filed 30 Dec 1903, decree issued 23 Mar 1904.
  [Ed. Note: Mark Moore (black), divorcee (age 50), married Louisa McComas (black) on 19 Nov 1904 in Harford County].

MOORE, MARY LOUISA vs. MOORE, ALEXANDER
  Case #2934, complaint filed 9 Jun 1879, decree issued 8 Apr 1880.

MOORE, MARTHA, see "Collins, Martha vs. James"

MORGAN, BENJAMIN vs. MORGAN, DOROTHEA AGNES
  Case #3938, complaint filed 31 Jan 1889, decree issued 22 Mar 1889.
MORRIS, REBECCA J., see "Salzig, Rebecca vs. Peter"
MOSES, EVA, see "Cole, Eva vs. Archer"
MOULTON, EFFIE, see "Murphy, James vs. Mary"
MURPHEY, MARY E., see "Wilson, William vs. Mary"
MURPHY, HESTER A. vs. MURPHY, JOHN B.
  Case #1303, "by her next friend Eliza Barnes"
  Complaint filed 2 Jun 1858, decree issued 28 Apr 1859.
MURPHY, JAMES H. vs. MURPHY, MARY V.
  Case #5991, complaint filed 3 Apr 1903, decree issued 23 Oct 1905.
  [Ed. Note: James H. Murphy (black) married Mary V. Thomas (black)
  on 3 May 1894. James H. Murphy, divorcee (age 33), married second
  to Effie Moulton on 12 Dec 1905; both times in Harford County].
MURPHY, JOHN T. vs. MURPHY, MARY A.
  Case #6398, complaint filed 28 Aug 1906, but no decree was noted.
  [Ed. Note: John T. Murphy married Mary A. Kenly by license dated
  18 Feb 1879 in Harford County].
MURPHY, SARAH, see "Roberts, William vs. Sarah" and also see
  "Roberts, Sarah vs. William"
NORRIS, SUSAN E. vs. NORRIS, JOHN W.
  Case #2634, complaint filed 12 May 1876, decree issued 21 Dec 1876.
  [Ed. Note: John W. Norris married Susan E. Billingslea by license
  dated 14 Jan 1860 in Harford County].
ONION, MARY E., see "Bavington, James vs. Mary"
ORSBURN, CLARA, see "Vogts, Herman vs. Mary"
OSBORN, SARAH E., see "Hicks, Sarah vs. James"
OSBORNE, IRENE vs. OSBORNE, BENJAMIN
  Case #6289, complaint filed 14 Oct 1905, decree issued 14 Mar 1908.
  [Ed. Note: Benjamin Osborne (black) married Irene Chambers (black)
  on 7 Aug 1902 in Harford County].
PALMER, CHARLES E. vs. PALMER, MARY
  Case #3295, complaint filed 16 Oct 1883, decree issued 20 Jun 1884.
  [Ed. Note: Charles Palmer married Mary Hoopman by license dated
  29 Jul 1877 in Harford County].
PALMER, VICTORIA B. vs. PALMER, JOHN
  Case #2487, complaint filed 18 Sep 1874, decree issued 2 Oct 1874.
  [Ed. Note: John Palmer, Jr. married Victoria Billingslea by license
  dated 16 Jan 1859 in Harford County].
PARKER, WILLIAM A. vs. PARKER, CORA C.

Case #6027, complaint filed 31 Aug 1903, decree issued 2 Nov 1903.
[Indicated "Cora C. Parker also now known as Cora C. Preston"].
PARMER, ELIZABETH, see "Brown, Jehu vs. Elizabeth"
PEACO, JAMES F. vs. PEACO, ANNIE
  Case #6698, complaint filed 29 Jun 1909, decree issued 25 Sep 1911.
  [Ed. Note: James F. Peaco (black) married Annie W. Wilmore (black)
  in Harford County on 15 Oct 1888. The index indicated that his name
  was "Peaco," but the record of marriage listed his name as "Peaker"].
PENNINGTON, ABBIE M., see "Griffith, Abbie vs. William"
PINION, MARY M. vs. PINION, PHILIP S.
  Case #6994, complaint filed 13 Mar 1912, decree issued 2 Dec 1912.
  [Ed. Note: Philip Pinion (black) married Mary M. Webster (black) in
  Harford County on 2 Oct 1890].
PONTIER, ELIZABETH H. vs. PONTIER, CHARLES E.
  Case #6770, complaint filed 24 Mar 1910, but no decree was noted.
  [Ed. Note: Charles Eugene Pontier married Elizabeth Helen Hoffman
  in Harford County on 22 Apr 1906].
PORTER, JOHN C., see "Fisher, Harry vs. Mary"
POTEET, JAMES vs. POTEET, MARGARET
  State of Maryland's High Court of Chancery granted a divorce to
  James Poteet from Margaret Poteet on 9 Mar 1829. (This case is not
  listed in the equity docket book for Harford County).
PRESTON, ANNA B., see "Hanna, J. Howard vs. Anna Belle"
PRESTON, CORA C., see "Parker, William vs. Cora"
PRESTON, JOHN W. vs. PRESTON, SARAH ANN
  Case #3728, complaint filed 8 Mar 1887, but no decree was noted.
  [Ed. Note: John W. Preston married "Sallie" Hall by license dated
  25 Nov 1876 in Harford County. No race was stated in the marriage
  record, but the equity docket book indicated they were "colored"].
PRESTON, MARIAN J. vs. PRESTON, SAMUEL
  Case #5492, complaint filed 27 Apr 1899, decree issued 17 May 1899.
  [Ed. Note: Samuel Preston married Marian Burgess in Harford County
  on 15 Apr 1886].
PRICE, RACHEL S. vs. PRICE, JOHN
  Case #791, complaint filed 1 Feb 1847, decree issued 18 Mar 1847.
PRIGG, DEVEREUX S. vs. PRIGG, E. BONNIE
  Case #6101, complaint filed 5 Apr 1904, decree issued 3 Sep 1904.
PRIGG, MARGARY ANN vs. PRIGG, ALLEN J.
  Case #2355, complaint filed 31 Jul 1873, but no decree was noted.
PYLE, DAISY H., see "Jones, Jacob vs. Daisy"

RANDOW, ELIZABETH vs. RANDOW, FREDERICK
  Case #5550, complaint filed 21 Nov 1899, decree issued 6 Dec 1899.
  [Ed. Note: Frederick John Randow (age 22) married Rachel Elizabeth
  White, widow (age 40), in Harford County on 16 Jan 1889].
RAY, EDNA G. vs. RAY, EUGENE A.
  Case #6171, complaint filed 26 Oct 1904, but no decree was noted.
  [Ed. Note: Eugene A. Ray (black), of Baltimore City, married Edna
  G. Lyle (black) in Harford County on 15 Apr 1903].
REED, ANDREW B. vs. REED, E. VIRGINIA
  Case #6607, complaint filed 13 Aug 1908, dismissed 29 Jun 1909.
  [Ed. Note: Andrew Reed married E. Virginia Davis on 10 May 1905
  in Harford County].
REED, E. VIRGINIA vs. REED, ANDREW B.
  Case #6932, complaint filed 30 Aug 1911, decree issued 20 Nov 1911.
  [Ed. Note: Andrew Reed married E. Virginia Davis. See above case].
REED, ELLA, see "Brown, Isaac vs. Eliza"
REYNOLDS, IDA, see "Wilgis, Vaunn vs. Ida"
REYNOLDS, LUDORA vs. REYNOLDS, JOHN A.
  Case #6325, complaint filed 21 Feb 1906, decree issued 12 Jun 1906.
RICA, FREDERICKA, see "Swob, George vs. Frederika"
RICE, ELLA, see "Brown, Isaac vs. Eliza"
RIGDON, JOHN A. vs. RIGDON, MYRA S.
  Case #6596, complaint filed 22 Jun 1908, decree issued 11 Jan 1909.
  [Ed. Note: John A. Rigdon married Myra S. Carr in Harford County
  on 17 Apr 1890].
RILEY, ALICE vs. RILEY, JOHN
  Case #5398, "by her next friend William T. Ely"
  Complaint filed 27 Apr 1898, decree issued 22 Jul 1898.
RILEY, STEVENSON A. vs. RILEY, GRACE V.
  Case #6908, complaint filed 28 Jun 1911, but no decree was noted.
  An entry in the equity docket book mentioned Baltimore County.
  [Ed. Note: Stephen (sic) Riley married Grace V. Ritchey on 19 Nov
  1896 in Harford County].
RINGGOLD, ELIZA A. vs. RINGGOLD, W. EMORY
  Case #3254, complaint filed 30 Apr 1883, decree issued 10 Nov 1883.
  [Ed. Note: Emory Ringgold married Eliza A. Lewis by license dated
  3 Jul 1867; Emory W. Ringold (sic) married Susan A. Hollingsworth
  by license dated 29 Apr 1886; both times in Harford County].
RITCHEY, GRACE V., see "Riley, Stevenson vs. Grace"
ROBERTS, ELLEN, see "Legoe, Salathiel vs. Elizabeth"

ROBERTS, SARAH vs. ROBERTS, WILLIAM JONES
   Case #6083, complaint filed 29 Feb 1904, but no decree was noted.
   [Ed. Note: William J. Roberts married Sarah Murphy on 23 Oct 1901
   in Harford County. See next case below].
ROBERTS, WILLIAM J. vs. ROBERTS, SARAH
   Case #6316, complaint filed 30 Jan 1906, decree issued 23 Oct 1906.
   [Ed. Note: William Roberts married Sarah Murphy. See above case].
ROBINSON, DANIEL vs. ROBINSON, SADIE
   Case #5395, complaint filed 21 Apr 1898, decree issued 11 Jul 1898.
   It also indicated "Sadie Robinson sometimes called Sadie Jamison."
   [Ed. Note: Daniel Robinson (black) married Sarah Ann Jemmison
   (black) on 2 Apr 1888 in Harford County].
ROBINSON, LILLIE, see "Bradfield, M. Lillian vs. Robert"
ROBINSON, LIZZIE, see "Brophy, Hanna E. vs. Dennis"
ROBINSON, MARY F. vs. ROBINSON, RICHARD
   Case #3992, complaint filed 15 Jun 1889, but no decree was noted.
   [Ed. Note: Richard Robinson, widower (age 56), married Mary
   Foreman in Harford County on 25 May 1887].
ROBINSON, RICHARD B. vs. ROBINSON, MARGARET
   Case #1536, complaint filed 12 Dec 1861, decree issued 23 Feb 1863.
   [Ed. Note: Richard H. *(sic)* Robinson married Margaret Jane Gray
   on 21 Aug 1852, as reported in the *Baltimore Sun* on 4 Sep 1852].
ROUSE, SARAH, see "Samuel H. Birckhead vs. Jane T."
RUSSELL, CARRIE, see "Schofield, Isaac vs. Carrie"
RUSSELL, S. SUSIE vs. RUSSELL, FRANK A.
   Case #5319, complaint filed 21 Jul 1897, decree issued 26 Oct 1897.
RUTLEDGE, LABAN L. vs. RUTLEDGE, EMMA L.
   Case #4663, complaint filed 8 Mar 1892, but no decree was noted.
   [Ed. Note: Laban L. Rutledge married Emma L. Rutledge on 30 Apr
   1890 in Harford County. The marriage index listed his first name as
   "Lealan" and the record of marriage listed it as "Leaban"].
RUTLEDGE, PENELOPE, see "Welch, Penelope vs. William"
SALZIG, REBECCA J. vs. SALZIG, PETER C.
   Case #4013, complaint filed 12 Aug 1889, decree issued 12 Dec 1889.
   [Ed. Note: Peter C. Salzig married Rebecca J. Morris by license dated
   30 Dec 1885 in Harford County].
SAUNDERS, SARAH A., see "Cunningham, Martha vs. Mortimer"
SAUNDERS, SARAH R., see "Grafton, Sarah vs. Joseph"
SCARBOROUGH, MARY, see "Dilworth, Mary vs. James"
SCHIRLING, LIDA B. vs. SCHIRLING, MICHAEL J.

Case #6704, complaint filed 9 Aug 1909, decree issued 16 Oct 1911.
[Ed. Note: Michael J. Schirling married Lidy Bodt in Harford County on 16 Oct 1901].

SCHOFIELD, ISAAC H. vs. SCHOFIELD, CARRIE A.
Case #6249, complaint filed 16 Jun 1905, but no decree was noted.
[Ed. Note: I. Henry Schofield married Carrie Russell on 14 Aug 1889 in Harford County. The index looks like "J. Henry," but it is actually "I. Henry," which would make his full name Isaac Henry Schofield].

SCHULTZ, WILLIAM, see "Evans, Murrell vs. Mamie Pearl"

SCHWAMB, CHARLES vs. SCHWAMB, ELLEN
Case #3921, complaint filed 16 Jan 1889, decree issued 20 Apr 1889.
[Ed. Note: Charles Schwamb married Ellen Wilson in Harford County on 10 Oct 1889].

SCOTT, MARY vs. SCOTT, JOHN E.
Case #6256, complaint filed 6 Jul 1905, decree issued 28 Feb 1906.
[Ed. Note: John E. Scott (black) married Mary Watters (black) on 2 Nov 1893 in Harford County].

SHARON, MARGARET H. vs. SHARON, JOHN H.
Case #6274, complaint filed 12 Sep 1905, decree issued 2 Oct 1905.
[Ed. Note: It is interesting to note that a John Henry Sharon (Sharnon?) married Mary Grace Davis (third cousins) in Harford County on 2 Feb 1897. Additional research will be necessary before drawing conclusions].

SHAW, CHARLES W. vs. SHAW, FRANCES H.
Case #6725, complaint filed 9 Oct 1909, dismissed 22 Oct 1909.

SHAW, FANNIE B. vs. SHAW, CHARLES W.
Case #6733, complaint filed 23 Nov 1909, but no decree was noted.

SHAY, ELLA M. vs. SHAY, WILLIAM S.
Case #4519, complaint filed 13 Feb 1893, dismissed(?) 28 Feb 1893.

SHAY, GEORGE A. vs. SHAY, STELLA M.
Case #6501, complaint filed 31 Jul 1907, but no decree was noted.
[Ed. Note: George Shay married Stella Moffett in Harford County on 25 Nov 1891].

SHIPLEY, SADIE C. vs. SHIPLEY, ALBERT E.
Case #5919, complaint filed 21 Jul 1902, decree issued 9 Oct 1902.
[Ed. Note: Albert Shipley married Sadie Johnson in Harford County on 11 Jan 1898].

SHURE, GEORGIA vs. SHURE, HENRY W.
Case #5692, complaint filed 27 Dec 1900, but no decree was noted.

SILK, MARY C. vs. SILK, JOHN
Case #5485, complaint filed 4 Apr 1899, dismissed 9 May 1899.

28

[Ed. Note: John Silk married Mary C. Larue in Harford County by license dated 27 Nov 1893].

SILVER, HANNAH K. vs. SILVER, JOHN A.
   Case #2195, complaint filed 16 Jan 1872, but no decree was noted.
   [Ed. Note: An entry in the docket mentioned Wilmington, Delaware].

SILVER, WILLIAM J. vs. SILVER, SALLIE
   Case #4602, complaint filed 28 Oct 1893, decree issued 25 Aug 1894.

SIMMS, SALLIE E. vs. SIMMS, JAMES L.
   Case #5847, complaint filed 10 Jan 1902, decree issued 16 Jun 1902.

SIMS, LAURA FRANCES vs. SIMS, RUSH F.
   Case #4475, complaint filed 23 Sep 1892, decree issued 13 Jan 1893.

SKILLMAN, ANNIE E. vs. SKILLMAN, FRANKLIN D.
   Case #3253, complaint filed 17 Apr 1883, decree issued 6 Aug 1883.
   [Ed. Note: Franklin D. Skillman married Anna E. Baumgart by license dated 13 Mar 1878 in Harford County].

SLADE, ELIZABETH A. vs. SLADE, THOMAS M.
   Case #4616, complaint filed 7 Dec 1893, decree issued 29 Mar 1894.

SMITH, ANNIE, see "Bond, Nannie vs. Lennox"

SMITH, ELIZABETH vs. SMITH, PETER
   Case #6300, complaint filed 7 Nov 1905, decree issued 20 Feb 1906.

SMITH, EMMA E. vs. SMITH, ROBERT T.
   Case #6371, complaint filed 18 Jun 1906, dismissed(?) 3 May 1907.
   Case #6740, complaint filed 13 Dec 1909, but no decree was noted.

SMITH, EMMA MABEL vs. SMITH, HARRY M.
   Case #6749, complaint filed 1 Feb 1910, discontinued 3 Jun 1911.
   Case #6832, complaint filed 3 Nov 1910, dismissed 30 Oct 1911.

SMITH, HANNAH, see "Hill, Hannah vs. Ralph"

SMITH, MARGARET, see "Tippett, Samuel vs. Margaret"

SMITH, REBECCA, see "Bevans, John vs. Rebecca"

SMITH, WILLIAM ABRAHAM vs. SMITH, LOUISE C.
   Case #5676, complaint filed 2 Nov 1900, but no decree was noted.
   [Ed. Note: This may be the Abraham Smith who married Louisa Fink in Harford County on 16 Feb 1885. Additional research will be needed to document if this was the same couple listed in the equity docket].

SMITH, WILLIAM A. vs. SMITH, R. HELEN
   Case #5935, complaint filed 15 Feb 1902, dismissed 6 Mar 1906.
   Case #6489, complaint filed 30 May 1907, decree issued 15 Jun 1907.
   [Ed. Note: William Smith married Helen Jewens in Harford County on 26 Sep 1901].

SMITH, WILLIAM E. vs. SMITH, SUSAN J.

Case #5271, complaint filed 9 Apr 1897, decree issued 17 Jul 1897.

SMITHSON, MARY, see "Smithson, Thomas vs. Lucretia"

SMITHSON, THOMAS P. vs. SMITHSON, LUCRETIA

Case #1129, complaint filed 27 Mar 1854, but no decree was noted in the equity docket book. [Ed. Note: The divorce was apparently granted. Thomas Poteet Smithson had married Lucretia Bosley by license dated 12 Feb 1849 in Harford County. He married second Mary Bull Smithson on 5 Jun 1859 and she died on 31 Jul 1864. Thomas married third to Mary Elizabeth Smithson on 9 Mar 1865. Lucretia Smithson, of Baltimore County, changed her name legally back to Lucretia Bosley by court order dated 18 Jan 1860].

SNYDER, MARGARETE, see "Swenson, Anders vs. Margaret"

SPATH, EMILY VIOLA vs. SPATH, JOHN HENRY

Case #5630, complaint filed 24 Jul 1900, but no decree was noted. [Also stated "John Henry Spath sometimes called John W. Bower"].

SPENCER, ANNIE, see "Cox, Annie vs. Benjamin"

SPENCER, FRANCES E., see "Brown, Eliza vs. Thaddeus"

SPRIGGS, WILLIAM H. vs. SPRIGGS, MARY

Case #6379, complaint filed 11 Jul 1906, but no decree was noted. [Ed. Note: William Spriggs married Mary Harris in Harford County on 29 Aug 1877].

STACKHOUSE, LILLIE M. vs. STACKHOUSE, WILLIAM H.

Case #3147, complaint filed 6 Feb 1882, but no decree was noted.

STANDIFORD, ALICE, see "Lee, Alice vs. William"

STERLING, WILLIAM F. vs. STERLING, SARAH ELIZABET

Case #4755, complaint filed 17 Oct 1894, decree issued 16 Aug 1898.

STEWART, ALEXANDER vs. STEWART, HANNAH J.

Case #6556, complaint filed 24 Mar 1908, but no decree was noted. Case #6884, complaint filed 18 Apr 1911, but no decree was noted. [Ed. Note: Alexander Stewart (black) married Hannah Hall (black) in Harford County by license dated 30 Apr 1900].

STEWART, MARY A. vs. STEWART, HENRY CLAY

Case #5636, complaint filed 1 Aug 1900, but no decree was noted. [Ed. Note: An entry in the docket book mentioned Baltimore City]. Case #6575, complaint filed 7 May 1908, decree issued 19 Sep 1908. [Ed. Note: This appears to be the Henry Stewart who married Mary Baldwin Harford County on 7 Sep 1871. Additional research will be necessary before drawing conclusions].

STINCHCOMB, LUCRETIA V. vs. STINCHCOMB, GEORGE W.

Case #6787, complaint filed 4 May 1910, decree issued 19 Jun 1911.

STINE, GEORGE vs. STINE, MARY

  Case #4440, complaint filed 23 May 1892, decree issued 21 Feb 1893.
  [Ed. Note: George Stine married Mollie A. Jordan in Harford County
  on 5 May 1869. See the next case below].

STINE, MARY A. vs. STINE, GEORGE

  Case #3535, complaint filed 2 Nov 1885, dismissed 8 Jan 1886.
  [Ed. Note: George Stine married Mollie A. Jordan. See above case].

STINE, MARY C. vs. STINE, THEODORE

  Case #6008, complaint filed 28 May 1903, decree issued 24 Aug 1903.

STITTARTT, FLORANCE, see "McCall, Thomas vs. Florence"

STOCKHAM, MARY E., see "Michael, James vs. Margaret"

STOVALL, OLIVIA G. vs. STOVALL, JOHN

  Case #5936, complaint filed 17 Sep 1902, decree issued 8 Jul 1903.

STREETT, RUTH E., see "McAtee, Ruth vs. Thomas"

STRONG, DEBORAH vs. STRONG, WILLIAM H.

  Case #6663, complaint filed 29 Mar 1909, decree issued 11 Jan 1910.
  [Ed. Note: William Strong married Debbie Baldwin on 7 May 1899 in
  Harford County. Deborah Strong, divorcee (age 37), married second
  to Alexander Bradford (age 27) on 29 Feb 1910 in Harford County].

STUBBS, EDWARD P. vs. STUBBS, FLORENCE K.

  Case #7071, complaint filed 28 Oct 1912, decree issued 30 Dec 1912.

STUMP, MAMIE vs. STUMP, ELMER

  Case #6492, complaint filed 13 Jun 1907, decree issued 10 Sep 1907.
  [Ed. Note: Elmer Stump (black) married Mamie Gray (black) on 19 Dec
  1896, and Mamie Stump, divorcee (age 32), married George Harris on
  12 Sep 1909; both times in Harford County].

SWARP, GEORGE, see "Swob (Swab), George vs. Frederika"

SWENSON, ANDERS A. vs. SWENSON, MARGARET E.

  Case #5960, complaint filed 27 Jan 1903, decree issued 21 Apr 1903.
  [Ed. Note: Anders J. Alfred Swensson (sic), of Baltimore County,
  married first to Margarete (sic) E. Snyder on 5 Nov 1891; Anders J.
  Alfred Swenson (sic), divorced (age 34), married second to Mary
  Anna Billmeyer on 5 Aug 1903; both times in Harford County].

SWIFT, ROBERT E. vs. SWIFT, CARRIE V.

  Case #6512, complaint filed 24 Sep 1907, decree issued 16 Mar 1908.
  [Ed. Note: Robert Swift, widower (age 50), married Carrie McCann in
  Harford County by license dated 10 Mar 1902].

SWOB (SWAB), GEORGE vs. SWOB (SWAB), FREDERIKA

  Case #1800, complaint filed 28 Aug 1867, but no decree was noted.
  Case #2507, complaint filed 20 Nov 1874, decree issued 16 Jun 1875.

[Ed. Note: George Swarp *(sic)* married Fredericka Rica by license dated 23 Aug 1864 in Harford County].

TAYLOR, CLARA B. vs. TAYLOR, HENRY L.
Case #3286, complaint filed 28 Aug 1883, but no decree was noted.
[Ed. Note: Henry L. Taylor married Clara B. Ackerman by license dated 11 May 1881 in Harford County].

TAYLOR, ANNIE S., see "McFadden, Annie vs. Otis"

TAYLOR, LATETIA, see "Watters, Letitia vs. William"

TAYLOR, MARY E., see "Welch, Theodore vs. Mary"

TAYLOR, SARAH A. vs. TAYLOR, ROBERT G.
Case #1733, complaint filed 26 Jul 1866, decree issued 13 Nov 1866.
[Ed. Note: Robert G. Taylor married Sarah A. Deaver by license dated 16 Aug 1862 in Harford County].

TAYSON, DANIEL J. vs. TAYSON, ETTA
Case #6141, complaint filed 18 Aug 1904, dismissed 6 Sep 1904.
Case #6154, same case, same dates, and no decree was noted.
[Ed. Note: Daniel Tayson married Etta Duff in Harford County on 22 Jan 1890].

TEMPLE, BENJAMIN F. vs. TEMPLE, ALICE
Case #6776, complaint filed 7 Apr 1910, decree issued 3 Aug 1910.
[Ed. Note: Benjamin Temple, divorcee (age 29), married Catherine Swift Lee on 4 Aug 1910 in Harford County]. Also, an entry in the equity docket book mentioned Baltimore City.

THALMAN, FRED B. vs. THALMAN, DORA V.
Case #6903, complaint filed 13 Jun 1911, dismissed(?) 22 Sep 1911.
[Ed. Note: Frederick B. Thalman married Dora V. Moffett in Harford County on 17 Apr 1895].

THOMAS, ARTHUR, see "Bay, Laura vs. William"

THOMAS, MARY, see "Murphy, James vs. Mary"

THOMPSON, WILLIAM M. vs. THOMPSON, ELIZABETH
Case #6523, complaint filed 5 Dec 1907, but no decree was noted.
[Ed. Note: William Thompson married Elizabeth Evans in Harford County on 24 May 1904].

TILLMAN, EMMA J., see "Fletcher, Emma vs. Moses"

TIPPETT, SAMUEL C. vs. TIPPETT, MARGARET L.
Case #6250, complaint filed 16 Jun 1905, decree issued 14 Oct 1905.
[Ed. Note: Samuel Tippett married Margaret Smith in Harford County on 27 Aug 1902].

TODD, MARY ANN, vs. TODD, JOHN T.
State of Maryland's High Court of Chancery granted a divorce to Mary

Ann Todd from John T. Todd on 5 Mar 1839. (This case is not listed in the equity docket for Harford County).
[Ed. Note: John Todd married Mary Ann Wood in Harford County by license dated 15 Nov 1836].

TONEY, GEORGEANNA vs. TONEY, GEORGE H.
Case #6513, complaint filed 22 Oct 1907, decree issued 24 Dec 1907.
[Ed. Note: George Tony *(sic)* married Georgeanna White in Harford County on 2 Oct 1887].

TROUTNER, MARY E. vs. TROUTNER, WILLIAM A.
Case #6942, complaint filed 27 Sep 1911, decree issued 20 Dec 1911.

TUCKER, NORA M. vs. TUCKER, HARRY C.
Case #5931, complaint filed 6 Sep 1902, dismissed(?) 6 Feb 1903.
Case #6217, complaint filed 25 Feb 1905, decree issued 1 Mar 1905.
[Ed. Note: Harry C.Tucker married Nora Vansant in Harford County on 28 Oct 1901].

TYDINGS, SALLIE A. vs. TYDINGS, THOMAS J.
Case #4799, complaint filed 4 Jan 1895, but no decree was noted.

VANBIBBER, GEORGE L., see "Hanna, Edith vs. J. Howard"

VANSANT, NORA, see "Tucker, Nora vs. Harry"

VISSAGE, NANCY vs. VISSAGE, JAMES
State of Maryland's High Court of Chancery "annulled control of" James Vissage over Nancy Vissage, of Harford County, on 28 Jan 1826 and ordered that she was to have custody of their child. (This case is not listed in the equity docket book for Harford County).

VOGTS, HERMAN C. vs. VOGTS, MARY C.
Case #6739, complaint filed 13 Dec 1909, dismissed(?) 18 Feb 1910.
[Ed. Note: Herman Vogts married Clara Orsburn in Harford County by license dated 26 Sep 1904. Also see the next case below].

VOGTS, MARY C. vs. VOGTS, HERMAN C.
Case #6860, complaint filed 23 Feb 1911, but no decree was noted.
[Ed. Note: Herman Vogts married Clara Orsburn. See above case].

WADE, ASIA vs. WADE, STEWART
Case #5480, complaint filed 16 Mar 1899, decree issued 29 Sep 1899.
[Ed. Note: Steward *(sic)* Wade married Asia Hall on 3 Jan 1888 in Harford County].

WALBECK, HENRY D. vs. WALBECK, LENA M. D.
Case #6912, complaint filed 10 Jul 1911, dismissed 3 Oct 1912.
[Ed. NoteL Henry D. Walbeck, of Jarrettsville, Maryland, married Lena Mernervia Daughton, of Delta, Pennsylvania, on 14 Mar 1910 in Harford County, Maryland].

WALKER, ALONZO (ALONZA) R. vs. WALKER, MARY ANN
  Case #4678, complaint filed 9 Apr 1894, dismissed(?) 28 May 1894.
  Case #5378, complaint filed 4 Mar 1898, decree issued 20 Jun 1899.
  [Ed. Note: Alonzo Walker married Mollie McEwing on 1 Feb 1888 in
  Harford County].
WALKER, SARAH JANE vs. WALKER, JOSEPH B.
  Case #1814, "by her next friend Alexander M. Fulford"
  Complaint filed 13 Nov 1867, decree issued 18 May 1872
  [Ed. Note: Joseph R. *(sic)* Walker married Sarah Jane Harman by
  license dated 20 Dec 1861 in Harford County].
WALKER, SARAH L. vs. WALKER, THOMAS EDWARD
  Case #5923, complaint filed 11 Aug 1902, decree issued 6 Nov 1902.
  [Ed. Note: Thomas E. Walker (black), divorced (age 30), married
  Mary Logan by license dated 18 Nov 1902 in Harford County].
WALLIS, SAMUEL R. vs. WALLIS, MARY ANN
  Case #1841, complaint filed 4 Apr 1868, decree issued 21 May 1868.
WALSTRUM, FANNIE vs. WALSTRUM, JAMES E.
  Case #6065, complaint filed 3 Feb 1904, decree issued 13 Feb 1905.
  [Ed. Note: James Waltsrum, widower (age 33), married Fannie Hawkins
  in Harford County on 18 Apr 1898].
WALTER, BESSIE L. vs. WALTER, JOSEPH W.
  Case #6870, complaint filed 21 Mar 1911, dismissed 16 Jun 1914.
  [Ed. Note: An entry in the docket book mentioned Baltimore County].
WALTER, CATHERINE M. vs. WALTER, W. OLIVER
  Case #6034, complaint filed 24 Sep 1903, decree issued 14 Oct 1903.
WALTER, JOHN W. vs. WALTER, VIRGINIA E.
  Case #1954, complaint filed 28 Jun 1869, decree issued 12 Feb 1875.
  [Ed. Note: John W. Walters *(sic)* married Virginia E. Brainard on
  26 Jan 1865, as reported in the *Baltimore Sun* on 27 Jan 1865].
WARD, JOHN AND VIRGINIA, see "Young, Martha vs. Jeremiah"
WATERS, JOHN W. vs. WATERS, SARAH C.
  Case #2939, complaint filed 25 Jul 1879, decree issued 9 Nov 1880.
  [Ed. Note: John W. Waters married Sarah Bishop by license dated
  16 Feb 1875 in Harford County].
WATTERS, ANNIE, see "Marku, William vs. Henrietta"
WATTERS, LETITIA vs. WATTERS, WILLIAM H.
  Case #6129, complaint filed 15 Jul 1904, decree issued 26 Apr 1905.
  [Ed. Note: William Watters (black) married Latetia Taylor (black) in
  Harford County on 7 Sep 1891].
WEBSTER, MARY M., see "Pinion, Mary vs. Philip"

WEBSTER, NEALY E., see "Hilton, Alfred vs. Alice"

WELCH, PENELOPE vs. WELCH, WILLIAM
Case #628, complaint filed 18 Nov 1842, and there appears to have been a legal separation granted, but no final divorce was decreed. [Ed. Note: William Welch married Penelope K. Rutledge by license dated 17 Apr 1838 in Harford County].

WELCH, THEODORE H. vs. WELCH, MARY ELIZABETH
Case #3807, complaint filed 7 Jan 1888, but no decree was noted. [Ed. Note: The equity docket book listed her name as "Elizabeth E. or Mary E. Welch." Theodore H. Welch married Mary E. Taylor in Harford County on 22 Sep 1874].

WELLS, JAMES C. vs. WELLS, ANNIE
Case #4960, complaint filed 19 Aug 1895, decree issued 14 Sep 1896.

WELLS, JENNIE, see "Johnson, William vs. Jennie"

WELSH, SARAH, see "Keith, John vs. Sarah"

WERFELMAN, ANNIE E. vs. WERFELMAN, JOHN C.
Case #4851, complaint filed 14 Mar 1895, decree issued 7 May 1895.

WESTCOTT, AUGUSTA, see "Dorsey, Isaac vs. Augusta"

WHITE, GEORGEANNA, see "Toney, George vs. Georgeanna"

WHITE, RACHEL E., see "Randow, Elizabeth vs. Frederick"

WHITEFORD, JOSEPH S. vs. WHITEFORD, MARGARET J.
Case #6968, complaint filed 27 Dec 1911, decree issued 18 Mar 1912. [Ed. Note: Joseph S. Whiteford married Maggie J. Jones by license dated 24 Nov 1885 in Harford County].

WHITEFORD, MARGARET, see "Janney, Margaret vs. Asbury"

WHITEFORD, SARAH JANE, see "Amos, Henry vs. Sarah"

WILDER, MARY S. vs. WILDER, WILLIAM H.
Case #6404, complaint filed 5 Sep 1906, decree issued 18 Dec 1906. [Ed. Note: Mary S. Wilder, divorcee (age 45), of Forest Hill, MD, married John F. Higgins, widower (age 62), of Crittenden, Virginia on 1 Jan 1907 in Harford County, Maryland].

WILGIS, VAUNN EDWARD vs. WILGIS, IDA
Case #3772, complaint filed 5 Aug 1887, decree issued 24 Feb 1888. [Ed. Note: Van (sic) Wilgis married Ida Reynolds by license dated 13 Oct 1885 in Harford County].

WILLIAMS, ELLA, see "Hilton, Alfred vs. Alice"

WILLIAMS, PHOEBE vs. WILLIAMS, JOHN
Case #3132, complaint filed 14 Nov 1881, but no decree was noted. [Ed. Note: John Williams married Phoebe Hilton on 14 Jul 1881 in Harford County].

WILLIAMS, SAMUEL J. vs. WILLIAMS, SARAH
Case #5506, complaint filed 20 Jun 1899, decree issued 24 Jul 1899.
[Ed. Note: Samuel Williams (black) married Sarah Gibson (black) on
21 Dec 1893 in Harford County].

WILLIAMSON, WILLIAM T. vs. WILLIAMSON, MARY ELIZABETH
Case #6444. complaint filed 19 Jan 1907, but no decree was noted.

WILMER, WILLIAM H. vs. WILMER, CLARA J.
Case #5462, complaint filed 24 Jan 1899, decree issued 19 Apr 1899.

WILMORE, ANNIE M., see "Peaco, James vs. Annie"

WILSON, WILLIAM H. vs. WILSON, MARY E.
Case #1766, complaint filed 12 Feb 1867, decree issued 9 Mar 1867.
[Ed. Note: William H. Wilson married Mary E. Murphey by license
dated 9 Jan 1850 in Cecil County].

WINTERS, HELEN MILTON, see "Bond, Helen vs. Samuel"

WISE, MARY vs. WISE, DANIEL
Case #6911, complaint filed 10 Jul 1911, but no decree was noted.
[Ed. Note: Daniel Wise married Mary E. Legar on 14 Jun 1876 in
Harford County].

WOOD, MARY ANN, see "Todd, Mary Ann vs. John"

WOOLEN, HARRIOTT, see "Dorney, Harriet vs. Henry"

WRIGHT, BELLE, see "McCall, Thomas vs. Florence"

WRIGHT, MAGGIE L., see "Curry, Samuel vs. Martha"

WRIGHT, MARY, see "Busher, Mary vs. Nicholas"

WRIGHT, WILLIAM J. vs. WRIGHT, ANNIE F.
Case #6307, complaint filed 29 Nov 1905, decree issued 23 Oct 1906.
[Ed. Note: William James Wright married Annie Frances Dornak in
Harford County on 18 Oct 1897].

YOUMANS, FLORENCE A. vs. YOUMANS, GEORGE
Case #5973, complaint filed 19 Feb 1903, dismissed(?) 6 May 1903.
[Ed. Note: George Youmans, of Tuxeda Park, New York, married
Florence McCommons on 20 May 1897 in Harford County, MD].

YOUNG, MARTHA V. vs. YOUNG, JEREMIAH
Case #1559, complaint filed 7 Apr 1862, decree issued 18 Nov 1862.
[Ed. Note: Jerry Young married M. Virginia Ward, daughter of John,
on 26 Nov 1857, as reported in the *Baltimore Sun* on 28 Nov 1857].

YOUNG, MARY A. vs. YOUNG, J. HENRY
Case #3854, complaint filed 6 Jul 1888, decree issued 19 Jun 1890.

www.ingramcontent.com/pod-product-compliance
Lightning Source LLC
Chambersburg PA
CBHW080940030426